APR -- 2018

Dolores Huerta
Advocate for Women and Workers

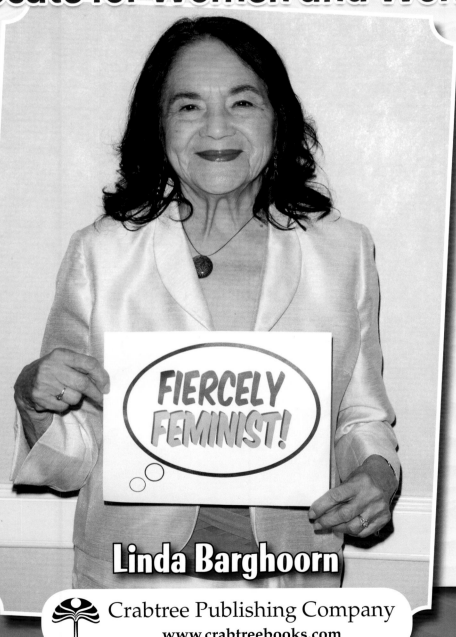

Linda Barghoorn

Crabtree Publishing Company
www.crabtreebooks.com

Author: Linda Barghoorn

Series research and development: Reagan Miller

Editorial director: Kathy Middleton

Editor: Crystal Sikkens

Proofreader: Wendy Scavuzzo

Photo researcher: Crystal Sikkens

Designer and prepress technician: Samara Parent

Print coordinator: Margaret Amy Salter

Photographs:

Alamy: © epa european pressphoto agency b.v.: page 20

Getty Images: © Beck Starr: title page; ©Arthur Schatz: page 15; © Cathy Murphy: pages 17, 22; © Valerie Macon: page 23; ©Carlos Chavez: page 24; © Al Schaben: page 25; © Alberto E. Rodriguez: page 26

Shutterstock.com: © ToskanaINC: pages 12-13; © Rena Schild: page 27 (top right); © Music4mix: page 30

The National Portrait Gallery: View of "One Life: Dolores Huerta," a 2015 exhibition at the National Portrait Gallery, Smithsonian Institution. Photo by Matailong Du: page 28

The Image Works: © 1976 George Ballis/Take Stock: pages 14, 16, 18, 19, 29

The Library of Congress: page 11

Wikimedia commons: © US Department of Labor: cover, pages 4-5; public domain: pages 6-7, 8-9, 10; © Gage Skidmore: page 21; © T. Murphy: pages 26-27 (bottom)

All other images from Shutterstock

About the author: Linda Barghoorn grew up in Fonthill, Ontario and attended Brock University in St. Catharines, where she graduated with a Bachelor of Arts in German. She spent twenty years living outside Canada – in Europe and the Middle East – during which time she began writing about and photographing her experiences. She is married with two grown daughters, and lives and works in Toronto, Canada.

Library and Archives Canada Cataloguing in Publication

Barghoorn, Linda, author
        Dolores Huerta : advocate for women and workers / Linda Barghoorn.

(Remarkable lives revealed)
Includes index.
Issued in print and electronic formats.
ISBN 978-0-7787-3418-5 (hardback).--
ISBN 978-0-7787-3422-2 (paperback).--ISBN 978-1-4271-1917-9 (html)

        1. Huerta, Dolores, 1930- --Juvenile literature. 2. Mexican American women labor leaders--Biography--Juvenile literature. 3. Women social reformers--United States--Biography--Juvenile literature. 4. Labor leaders--United States--Biography--Juvenile literature. 5. Social reformers--United States--Biography--Juvenile literature. I. Title.

HD6509.H84B37 2017   j331.88'13092   C2016-907095-6
                                                                          C2016-907096-4

Library of Congress Cataloging-in-Publication Data

CIP available at the Library of Congress.

Crabtree Publishing Company

www.crabtreebooks.com   1-800-387-7650

Printed in Canada/022017/CH20161214

Published in Canada
Crabtree Publishing
616 Welland Ave.
St. Catharines, Ontario
L2M 5V6

Published inthe United States
Crabtree Publishing
PMB 59051
350 Fifth Ave., 59th Floor
New York, NY 10118

Published in theUnited Kingdom
Crabtree Publishing
Maritime House
Basin Road North, Hove
BN41 1WR

Published in Australia
Crabtree Publishing
3 Charles Street
Coburg North
VIC, 3058

Contents

Dolores Huerta

Everyone has a story to share. These stories are known as biographies and they help us better understand each other and the world around us. Some people's stories might be well known, but others may not. Even a story that isn't well known can be remarkable and can inspire others. This is because everyone has different ideas of what makes someone remarkable. Many remarkable people show certain qualities such as commitment, sacrifice, and good values. As you read through Dolores Huerta's story, look for qualities in her that many people consider to be remarkable.

What Is a Biography?

A biography is the story of a person's life. We read biographies to learn about a person's experiences and thoughts. Biographies can be based on many sources of information. Primary sources include a person's own words or pictures. Secondary sources include friends, family, and media.

Dolores speaks at a ceremony honoring the Farm Workers Movement.

Activist and Role Model

Dolores Huerta (WEHR-tah) grew up in California's San Joaquin (San-wah-KEEN) Valley surrounded by many farm workers' families who lived in desperately poor conditions. She became determined to help them, and committed her life to providing dignity and justice for both farm workers and women. The strength and determination she showed throughout her struggle has made her a respected role model for many people.

? THINK ABOUT IT

Do you know someone remarkable? What qualities make them a remarkable person?

Early Influences

Dolores Huerta was born on April 10, 1930, in Dawson, New Mexico. Her family roots were in Mexico. When Dolores was three, her parents—Juan Fernandez (Fer-NAN-dez) and Alicia Chavez (CHAH-vez)—divorced. Dolores moved with her mother and two brothers to Stockton, California. They lived in a small farming community among poor immigrant families who came from many different countries.

Single Parent Family

Dolores grew up during a time known as the Great Depression. Dolores' mother struggled to hold two jobs just to make enough money to support her young family. Dolores's grandfather, Herculano (Hur-kyuh-LAH-noh), often took care of the children. Dolores adored him. He joked with her, calling her "seven tongues" because she talked so much. Although life was difficult, Dolores enjoyed a loving and happy family. Her mother and grandfather were very strong influences in her life.

The Great Depression

In 1929, the American **stock market** crashed. This meant people that bought stocks or shares in companies suddenly lost their life savings. Stores and factories closed and many people lost their jobs. Life was very difficult for many poor and middle-class families throughout the 1930's. This period was called The Great Depression.

This family lost their home in Phoenix, Arizona, during The Great Depression. They are walking to San Diego in hopes of finding better opportunities.

A Mother's Influence

Dolores's mother was a hard worker. Later, she bought a restaurant and a hotel. She always welcomed the low-wage farm **laborers** and treated them kindly, even when they couldn't afford to pay her. She was also active in the community church and local organizations. Dolores and her brothers shared chores at home and at their mother's business. Dolores was always treated as an equal at home. At the time, this was unusual for a girl. Dolores admired her mother's independence and **entrepreneurial** spirit. Alicia taught her the importance of treating everyone with respect.

> *I think my mother was a **feminist** for her time.*
>
> —Dolores Huerta, *AARP Magazine*, "Dolores Huerta: The Vision and Voice of Her Life's Work", 2004.

Distant Father Figure

After her parents' divorce, Dolores rarely saw her father. He worked in the coal mines and became a migrant worker picking crops. He was often frustrated by the poor working conditions and low wages. Determined to improve workers' rights, he joined a **labor union** and became a leader. Later, he gained a position in the New Mexico state government for one term. When Dolores was older, she reconnected with her father. His involvement in labor issues inspired her to become an **activist**.

? THINK ABOUT IT

How was Dolores influenced by her parents?

Coal mining was challenging and dangerous work. Workers often lost their lives in the mines.

Field Laborers

The town of Stockton was in the San Joaquin Valley—home to many fruit, vegetable, cotton, and cattle farms. Although farm owners ran successful businesses, the field laborers who worked for them were often very poor. Some of these laborers were migrant workers who came to pick the crops during harvest season. Although laws stated how farm laborers should be treated, many farm owners ignored them. Workers were often disrespected, mistreated, and poorly paid.

Workers weed a field of sugar beets.

Poor Working Conditions

Farm laborers worked long days in extreme heat and were exposed to dangerous chemicals. Their families lived in shacks with no heat, running water, or toilets. For their hard work, they often earned less than one dollar an hour. Migrant workers had even fewer rights. Many did not have legal status to work in America and risked being sent back to their country if the U.S. government found them. They could not get health insurance or **welfare** benefits if they lost their jobs or were injured.

Migrant Workers

Migrant workers are people who travel—sometimes to another country—to look for work. Often the work is seasonal and then they return home.

This was a typical migrant worker's home in the fields.

Inspiring an Activist

Dolores's mother worked hard to provide her children with music lessons and after-school activities. Dolores learned to play the violin and piano, and took dance lessons. As a student at Stockton High School, Dolores was popular, enthusiastic, and hardworking. She could speak English and Spanish. Like her mother, Dolores was also active in her community. She participated in school clubs and belonged to a Girl Scout troop. At her church, Dolores sang in the choir and belonged to the youth group.

While she was in high school, Dolores became a majorette. A majorette is someone who dances while twirling a baton, or thin stick. Majorettes often perform with marching bands in parades.

Discrimination

Unfortunately, it was in high school where Dolores says she felt **discrimination** for the first time. Several teachers were suspicious of her academic success. They believed that her Mexican-American background meant she wasn't as smart as other students. They felt she was incapable of achieving the same level of success that other non-**ethnic** students achieved. She was once accused of stealing another student's work. The prejudice that many Mexican immigrants frequently experienced came as a shock to young Dolores, who was accustomed to being treated as an equal.

? THINK ABOUT IT

Why did Dolores's high school teachers discriminate against her?

Short Teaching Career

Dolores graduated from high school in 1947 and continued her studies at the University of the Pacific's Delta College in Stockton, where she earned a teaching degree. She was the first person in her family to attend college. This was unusual for **Hispanic** women at the time. Most got married and stayed home to raise families. Dolores accepted a teaching job, but soon became frustrated by the poverty of the farm workers' children she was teaching, and her inability to help them.

> *I couldn't tolerate seeing kids come to class hungry and needing shoes. I thought I could do more by organizing farm workers than by trying to teach their hungry children.*
>
> **—Dolores Huerta, www.rollingstone.com**

After a short time teaching, Dolores resigned. She felt she could do more by helping the families of the children fight for better rights and living conditions.

The "Passionate One"

Dolores joined the Stockton chapter of the Community Service Organization (CSO). This was a Mexican-American group who supported local working-class families. There she met César (SAY-zar) Chávez, who shared her goal of helping the farm laborers. They made a great team. César was a lively leader, while Dolores was a talented organizer and negotiator. Her defiant style and tireless commitment earned her the nickname *La pasionaria* (pah-syo-NAH-ree-yah), or "the passionate one."

Dolores Huerta and César Chávez led the United Farm Workers movement.

Grassroots Beginning

The CSO was a grassroots, or newly created, group that encouraged the poorly educated farm laborers to become involved in political decisions that could improve their lives. Dolores helped run educational programs, organize **citizenship** classes, and register voters. She fought for improvements to neighborhood streets and parks. She worked to help laborers get access to government assistance when they were injured or unemployed. Her work was so successful that she was promoted to represent the CSO at the state level. No woman had held that position before.

> *We would say to the workers: You have power... you can make the difference.*
>
> —**Dolores Huerta,** *PBS News Hour* interview with Ray Suarez, 2012.

*Dolores's strong communication, **lobbying**, and bargaining skills were powerful tools that united laborers and inspired them to fight for change.*

Organizing a Movement

In 1962, César and Dolores left the CSO to create the National Farm Workers Association (NFWA), later known as the United Farm Workers (UFW). They wanted to organize farm laborers into unions that could fight for better working conditions. That was difficult because some workers were in the States illegally and had no rights to work there. Others were uneducated or didn't speak English.

Richard Chávez

Along with César Chávez and Dolores Huerta, Richard Chávez helped create the UFW. He and Dolores shared a long-term relationship and had four children together.

Dolores Huerta with Richard Chávez, César's brother.

The Grape Strike

Although farm laborers had won some legal rights, they were still treated poorly by most farm owners who ignored the laws. As NFWA members, the laborers decided to challenge the grape farm owners in Delano, California. They refused to work until the farm owners promised to guarantee their rights. This became known as the Delano Grape **Strike**. The farm owners worried about losing money as more laborers joined the strike. Some offered better wages and healthcare to their workers. But most refused to help the striking workers, and threatened those who helped organize them.

Dolores joins the striking farm workers in the Delano Grape Strike.

Boycott

Dolores encouraged consumers to join the fight by **boycotting** grapes. More than 14 million people joined the boycott when they learned about the poor working conditions that the farm laborers endured. After five years, the laborers reached an agreement with the farm owners. They were provided with healthcare benefits, toilets, and fresh running water, and were protected from dangerous **pesticides**. Dolores's organizing and negotiating skills were important in achieving this success. She was nicknamed Dolores *Huelga* (Huh-WELL-gah), Spanish for "strike."

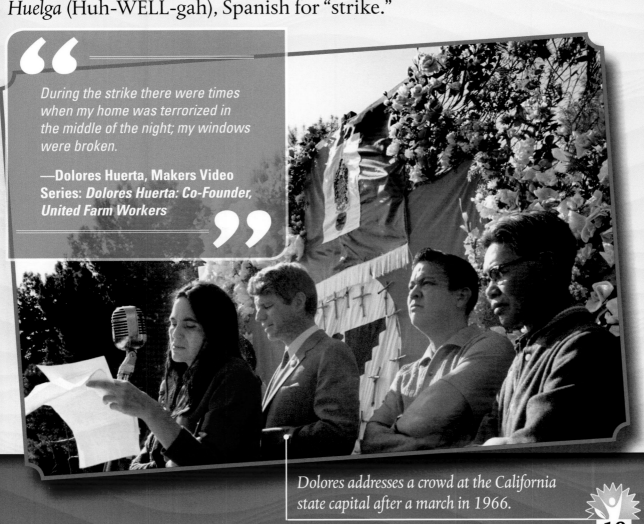

> " During the strike there were times when my home was terrorized in the middle of the night; my windows were broken.
>
> —**Dolores Huerta, Makers Video Series:** *Dolores Huerta: Co-Founder, United Farm Workers*

Dolores addresses a crowd at the California state capital after a march in 1966.

Farm Laborers' Rights

For the next two decades, Dolores continued to help organize the laborers. She visited farmers' fields, attended protest rallies, and negotiated in government offices. She helped achieve the first law allowing farm workers to organize and negotiate for their own rights. She lobbied constantly to gain **amnesty** for farm workers who had lived, worked, and paid taxes for years, but were denied the same rights as American citizens. This has led to the creation of an immigration law, which helped migrant workers obtain legal status to live and work in the United States.

Dolores takes part in a 2013 protest demanding changes to American immigration laws.

? THINK ABOUT IT

What rights did the new laws give the farm laborers?

Dolores speaks at a campaign rally for United States presidential candidate, Hillary Clinton.

Political Activism

Dolores has never been afraid to stand up for what she believes is right. She has been arrested more than twenty times during her career, often for refusing to obey the laws that hurt workers' rights. Once she was beaten so badly by a policeman at a political rally that she almost died. She has continued to fight for equality for everyone and to fight for laws that defend each individual's civil rights. In her later career, she became more involved in national politics and participated in several United States presidential campaigns.

Dolores Huerta (far right) joins the UFW Board of
Directors for a group portrait in the 1970s.

Fighting Stereotypes

Dolores is proud of her role as a *Chicana* (Chi-KAH-nuh)—a woman
of Mexican heritage. Throughout her life, she has fought gender
and ethnic **stereotypes**. Mexican-American women were expected
to dedicate themselves to raising a family. But Dolores stubbornly
embarked on a career that took place largely in a man's world. Her
authority was often challenged by men. Many did not like seeing a
woman—especially an ethnic woman—in power. Some refused to
negotiate with her, but Dolores refused to be intimidated.

A Strong Role Model

Without realizing it, Dolores had become a powerful role model for many women. They admired her strength and commitment to stand up for others. A meeting with well-known feminist Gloria Steinem (STY-nuhm) informed Dolores of the growing movement for women's rights. She began to include women's issues in her struggle for equality. She has encouraged women to look beyond their traditional family roles and pushed them to accept political positions within government. She continues to be a strong advocate for the rights of women and **Latinos**.

We, as women, have to put big lights around our accomplishments.

—Dolores Huerta, Makers Video Series: *Dolores Huerta: Co-Founder, United Farm Workers*

Dolores attends a California rally in 2014 to support human rights.

A Lifetime of Accomplishment

In 2002, Dolores Huerta was presented with a $100,000 Creative Citizenship Award. This generous prize allowed her to establish the Dolores Huerta Foundation. With the foundation, Dolores was able to continue her work to help improve the lives of women, children, and poor working-class families. Through its training and leadership programs, Dolores hopes to inspire the next generation of leaders to advocate for others.

> " Every moment is an organizing opportunity, every person a potential activist, every minute a chance to change the world.
>
> —**Dolores Huerta,**
> **www.changemakrs.com**

Dolores Huerta receives the 2002 Puffin/Nation Prize for creative citizenship.

Building Strong Communities

The foundation works to create stronger, wealthier communities. Dolores has always believed that the key to creating change in people's lives is to get them organized and involved. The foundation's work is built on this principle. It creates "united neighbors" groups in communities and selects individuals from these groups to be trained as leaders. These leaders identify problems in the community and partner with community members to find solutions.

? THINK ABOUT IT

What principle inspires the foundation's work?

Vecinos Unidos, or United Neighbors, presents a plaque to a police lieutenant for his service to a troubled California neighborhood.

Celebrating Dolores

Dolores Huerta's accomplishments have been celebrated in many ways—from slogans and portraits to public murals, movies, and museum exhibits. Her commitment to social change in America has earned her nine honorary degrees from American universities and countless awards. In 1984, the California State Senate presented her with an Outstanding Labor Leader Award. She has been inducted into the National Women's Hall of Fame, and has been celebrated as one of the 100 Most Important Women of the 20th Century. She also the subject of a recent documentary called "Woman in Motion."

In 2009, Dolores attended the IMAGEN awards, which celebrate Latinos' accomplishments.

Highest Honors

Dolores's dedication and commitment across borders have been acknowledged by the Mexican and American governments. In 1998, she received the Ohtli Award from the government of Mexico—the highest honor granted to a citizen living outside their country. It celebrated Dolores's life-long commitment and influence within the Latino community. In 2012, President Barack Obama presented Dolores with the Presidential Medal of Freedom. The award recognized Dolores's enduring contributions to American society.

The Presidential Medal of Freedom is the highest **civilian** award in the United States.

This mural on the First Avenue Bridge in Los Angeles, California, celebrates the accomplishments of Dolores Huerta. It was painted by Yreina Cervantez.

"One Life"

The Smithsonian Museum's National Portrait Gallery, in Washington D.C., tells the story of America's history and culture through its collection of portraits of influential individuals. In 2015, Dolores Huerta was recognized in its "One Life" series. This series has paid tribute to a variety of American citizens—from presidents to baseball players and military generals. The Smithsonian Museum was the first national museum to honor Dolores's accomplishments.

The "One Life" exhibition highlighted Dolores's role in the farm workers movement.

Sacrifice and Reward

Over the years, Dolores's demanding career and schedule often conflicted with her role as a mother. She loved her eleven children deeply and admits her family life was sometimes sacrificed for her career. But she also believes that her work demonstrated to them the importance of being a responsible, engaged citizen. Her union's motto *¡Si se puede!* or "Yes, you can do it!" has guided her work and been a philosophy for her growing children. She takes pride in their achievements as adults, some of whom have chosen to continue her work. Now in her 80s, Dolores remains an outspoken leader and activist.

After a meeting, Dolores and three of her children join Jim Drake and Julio Hernandez of the UFW in a folk song.

Personal Life

Dolores was married twice. She married Ralph Head in college and had two children with him. Later, while working at the UFW she married Ventura Huerta, with whom she had six children. Her last relationship was with Richard Chávez. They had four children together.

Writing Prompts

1. What personal skills and talents did Dolores use in her lobbying efforts to improve working conditions for the farm workers she supported?

2. How do you feel about the sacrifices Dolores made in her own family life to pursue her community work in support of poor farm workers and their families?

3. Dolores created the motto ¡*Si se puede!* ("Yes, you can do it!") which has guided her work and family life. Create a motto for you and your family to live by. What does your motto mean to you?

4. What are some of the key accomplishments Dolores achieved during her career in helping the farm workers?

Learning More

Books

Dolores Huerta: Voice for the Working Poor by Alex Van Tol. Crabtree Publishing Company, 2011.

Dolores Huerta: A Hero to Migrant Workers by Sarah Warren. Two Lions, 2012.

Dolores Huerta (Latinos in American History) by Becky Thatcher. Mitchell Lane Publishers, 2002.

Websites

http://doloreshuerta.org
A comprehensive website about the Dolores Huerta Foundation and its work.

http://recordsofrights.org/events/43/delano-grape-strike-and-boycott
An overview of the Delano Grape Strike and Boycott, with photographs.

http://npg.si.edu/exhibition/one-life-dolores-huerta
The National Portrait Gallery's overview of the *One Life: Dolores Huerta* exhibit at the Smithsonian Institute.

http://hs213.weebly.com/research.html
Brief history of Dolores Huerta's life, including a video about her receiving the Presidential Medal of Honor from President Obama.

Glossary

activist A person who uses or supports strong actions to help make changes in society

amnesty A decision not to punish someone for their crime, or to release a prisoner serving their sentence

boycott To refuse to buy, use, or participate in something as a way of protesting

civilian A person who is not a member of the military, police, or firefighting force

citizenship The status of being a citizen of a particular country

discrimination The practice of treating a person unfairly or differently from other people because of their race, gender, or religion

entrepreneurial Having the skills to start a new business and take risks to make money

ethnic Belonging to a particular race or group of people who have a culture that is different from the main culture of a country

feminist Someone who believes that men and women should have equal rights and opportunities

Hispanic Someone who comes from an area where Spanish is spoken

laborer Worker

labor union An organization of workers formed to protect the rights and interests of its members

Latino A person whose family is originally from South America, Central America, or Mexico

lobby To organize a group of people to work together to influence a government decision

migrant worker A person who travels to different places to find work

pesticide A chemical that is used to kill insects that damage crops

stereotype An unfair or untrue belief that people have about groups of people or things that share a particular characteristic

stock market The organized system for buying and selling shares, or parts, of companies

strike When workers refuse to work until an employer agrees to their demands

welfare A government program for poor or unemployed people that helps pay for their food, housing, or medicine

Index